SRA Open Court Reading

Decodable Takehome Books

Level D Set 1

A Division of The McGraw·Hill Companies

Columbus, Ohio

SRA/McGraw-Hill

A Division of The McGraw·Hill Companies

Copyright © 2000 by SRA/McGraw-Hill.

Printed in the United States of America.

Send all inquiries to:
SRA/McGraw-Hill
8787 Orion Place
Columbus, OH 43240-4027

ISBN 0-02-661054-X
6 7 8 9 MAL 04 03 02 01

Contents

About the Decodable Takehome Books

The *SRA Open Court Reading Decodable Books* allow your students to apply their knowledge of phonic elements to read simple, engaging texts. Each story supports instruction in a new phonic element and incorporates elements and words that have been learned earlier.

The students can fold and staple the pages of each *Decodable Takehome Book* to make books of their own to keep and read. We suggest that you keep extra sets of the stories in your classroom for the children to reread.

How to make a Decodable Takehome Book

1. Tear out the pages you need.

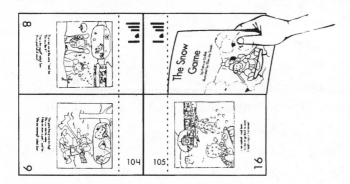

2. For 16-page stories, place pages 8 and 9, 6 and 11, 4 and 13, and 2 and 15 faceup.

or

2. For 8-page stories, place pages 4 and 5, and pages 2 and 7 faceup.

For 16-page book

3. Place the pages on top of each other in this order: pages 8 and 9, pages 6 and 11, pages 4 and 13, and pages 2 and 15.

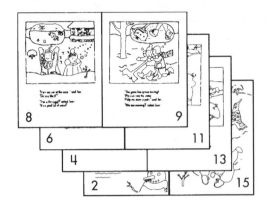

4. Fold along the center line.

5. Check to make sure the pages are in order.

6. Staple the pages along the fold.

For 8-page book

3. Place pages 4 and 5 on top of pages 2 and 7.

4. Fold along the center line.

5. Check to make sure the pages are in order.

6. Staple the pages along the fold.

Just to let you know...

A message from _____

Help your child discover the joy of independent reading with *SRA Open Court Reading*. From time to time your child will bring home his or her very own *Decodable Takehome Books* to share with you. With your help, these stories can give your child important reading practice and a joyful shared reading experience.

You may want to set aside a few minutes every evening to read these stories together. Here are some suggestions you may find helpful:

- Do not expect your child to read each story perfectly, but concentrate on sharing the book together.
- Participate by doing some of the reading.
- Talk about the stories as you read, give lots of encouragement, and watch as your child becomes more fluent throughout the year!

Learning to read takes lots of practice. Sharing these stories is one way that your child can gain that valuable practice. Encourage your child to keep the *Decodable Takehome Books* in a special place. This collection will make a library of books that your child can read and reread. Take the time to listen to your child read from his or her library. Just a few moments of shared reading each day can give your child the confidence needed to excel in reading.

Children who read every day come to think of reading as a pleasant, natural part of life. One way to inspire your child to read is to show that reading is an important part of your life by letting him or her see you reading books, magazines, newspapers, or any other materials. Another good way to show that you value reading is to share a *Decodable Takehome Book* with your child each day.

Successful reading experiences allow children to be proud of their new-found reading ability. Support your child with interest and enthusiasm about reading. You won't regret it!

Open Court
Reading

Casper and Chip

by Carolyn Crimi
illustrated by Kersti Frigell

A Division of *The McGraw-Hill Companies*

Columbus, Ohio

"There, Chip!" said Casper. "There is nothing left on your back. I will help you get up."

Chip got up. Then Chip and Casper crossed the river to home.

"Well, Chip," said Casper. "We have no silver, but I'd much rather be a poor man with you than a rich man without you!"

SRA/McGraw-Hill

A Division of The McGraw-Hill Companies

Copyright © 2000 by SRA/McGraw-Hill.

Send all inquiries to:
SRA/McGraw-Hill
8787 Orion Place
Columbus, OH 43240-4027

2

"There, Chip!" said Casper. "Now can you get up?"

Chip still could not get up. Casper took the silver rock out of his bag.

"There, Chip!" said Casper. "Now can you get up?"

Chip still did not get up. Casper took the silver box off his back.

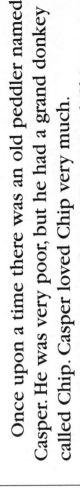

Once upon a time there was an old peddler named Casper. He was very poor, but he had a grand donkey called Chip. Casper loved Chip very much.

One day, on the way home, Casper and Chip stumbled upon a pot of silver in a ditch by the path.

"Look, Chip!" said Casper, looking at the silver.

Casper lifted the box onto Chip's back. But the box was too heavy. Poor Chip fell to the ground.

"Get up, Chip!" cried Casper. "We must cross the river to get this silver home!" But Chip could not get up. Casper took the pot of silver out of Chip's bag.

"This silver will make me a rich man!" Casper put the silver in Chip's bag and went on. In a little bit, Casper and Chip stumbled upon a silver rock as big as a man's hat. "Look, Chip!" said Casper. "This rock will make me a rich man!"

4

Casper put the rock in Chip's bag. The rock was heavy. Poor Chip plodded along.

A little later, Casper and Chip stumbled upon a solid silver box. "Look, Chip!" said Casper. "This box will make me a rich man!"

5

SRA Open Court Reading

The Red and Black Cap

by Caitlin McLeary
illustrated by Len Epstein

SRA

A Division of The McGraw-Hill Companies

Columbus, Ohio

13

"Dan has his cap back!" said Len.

"Yes," said Pat. "This is Dan's damp, red and black ball cap."

8

SRA/McGraw-Hill

A Division of The McGraw-Hill Companies

Copyright © 2000 by SRA/McGraw-Hill.

Printed in the United States of America.

Send all inquiries to:
SRA/McGraw-Hill
8787 Orion Place
Columbus, OH 43240-4027

"Let Dan have the cap," said Mr. Kam.

15

"Oh," said Mr. Kam, "a red and black ball cap!"

"Where?" asked Len.

3

"Oh!" said Pat. "Can Dan have that ball cap back?"

6

4

"There!" said Mr. Kam.
"I see the red and black cap," said Len.
"Pat the cap," said Mr. Kam.

"The cap is damp. It will mat," said Mr. Kam.
"This cap is bad."

5

Open Court Reading

Ben and the Cat

by Lucie Shephard
illustrated by Gary Undercuffler

SRA

A Division of The McGraw-Hill Companies

Columbus, Ohio

Ben sat on a box next to the cat.
Then the cat sat in Ben's lap. "Well," said Ben. "I guess I
have a new pet. I'll call you Scat."

SRA/McGraw-Hill

A Division of The McGraw-Hill Companies

Copyright © 2000 by SRA/McGraw-Hill.

All rights reserved. Except as permitted under the United States Copyright Act, no part of this publication may be reproduced or distributed in any form or by any means, or stored in a database or retrieval system, without prior written permission from the publisher.

Printed in the United States of America.

Send all inquiries to:
SRA/McGraw-Hill
8787 Orion Place
Columbus, OH 43240-4027

2

When Ben went to lock the pen, the cat ran after a rat, and Ben fell. "Scat, cat," said Ben. But the cat didn't scat.

7

18

Ben went to the big pen. There was a little cat in back of the big pen. The cat ran when Ben went to pet him.

3

When Ben went to get the hens, the cat ran after Ben's best hen. "Scat, cat," called Ben. But the cat didn't scat.

6

19

4

When Ben fed him, the cat had a nap in Ben's lap. "I'll let him eat food from a pan," Ben said.

When Ben went to tend to the pigs, the cat sat on Ben's cap. "Scat, cat," Ben said. But the cat didn't scat.

5

20

SRA Open Court Reading

Phil's Work

by Alvaro Ruiz
illustrated by Gary Undercuffler

SRA

A Division of The McGraw-Hill Companies

Columbus, Ohio

"Just watch, Pop," he'd say. "I'll have a plan that is not odd."

"Don't stop your odd plans, Phil," his pop would tell him as he got the ax. "But don't stop chopping logs."

8

SRA/McGraw-Hill

A Division of The McGraw-Hill Companies

Copyright © 2000 by SRA/McGraw-Hill.

All rights reserved. Except as permitted under the United States Copyright Act, no part of this publication may be reproduced or distributed in any form or by any means, or stored in a database or retrieval system, without prior written permission from the publisher.

Printed in the United States of America.

Send all inquiries to:
SRA/McGraw-Hill
8787 Orion Place
Columbus, OH 43240-4027

But when work hit bottom with a splash, Phil was not upset.

"It was an odd plan," he'd say. "Other work will come along."

23

Phil and his dad chopped logs with axes. They chopped in the hot sun.

"This is not a lot of fun," Phil said.

3

I've got it!
I'll help golfers!

Some of Phil's plans would drop with a plop.

6

Open Court
Reading

I've got it! Corncob dolls!

Phil wished for other work.
"Just watch, Pop," he said. "I'm going to be rich."
As he chopped thick logs, Phil had a plan for work.

4

When a job plan was wrong, Phil was not mad.
"It was an odd plan," he'd say. "Other work
will come along."

5

SRA Open Court Reading

Pets in Class

by Chris Meramec
illustrated by Thor Wickstrom

A Division of *The McGraw-Hill Companies*

Columbus, Ohio

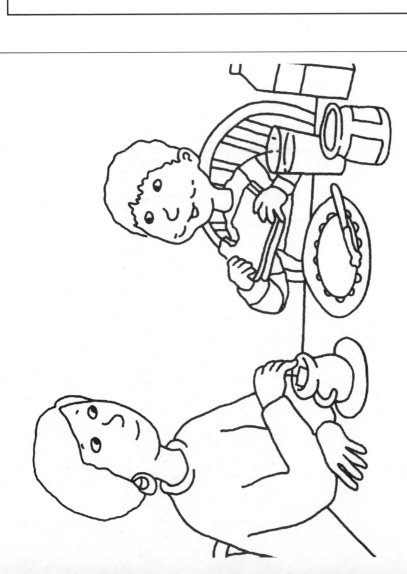

"The cats were skipping and hopping. The dogs were rushing at the cats. A bunch of pups ran and hid. A frog got away. What a mess!" said Mom. "I bet there will be no pets in class again!"

"That's what Ms. Kent said," said Bob.

16

SRA/McGraw-Hill

A Division of The McGraw-Hill Companies

Copyright © 2000 by SRA/McGraw-Hill.

Printed in the United States of America.

Send all inquiries to:
SRA/McGraw-Hill
8787 Orion Place
Columbus, OH 43240-4027

Ribbet!

This is wrong!

"Oh, not much. Todd got his frog back. Frogs do not come back when you ask them to," said Bob.

A Class Plan

"My dog has six pups," said Phil. "They are so much fun. They run and tumble. Then they nap in their soft bed."

"Have you met Hip-Hop?" asked Ann.

"Hip-Hop is Todd's pet frog."

3

"What else?" asked Mom.

14

"Lots of children have fun pets," said Bob.
"Ms. Kent, can we bring pets to class?" asked Phil.

4

"Yes. Phil's pups were running and dumping things.
Then the dogs ran, too. The dogs ran, the cats were
hopping, and the pups hid," said Bob.
"That's too bad!" said Mom.
"It was fun!" said Bob.

Catch the pups!

I got a pup!

13

28

"You can," said Ms. Kent. "But we must plan the things we will do."

5

"What next?" said Mom.

"I got to catch a pup," said Bob.

"You had to catch pups?" asked Mom.

12

1. Pet day Monday!
2. Get pets after lunch.
3. Pets must have a tag.
4. Some pets can be in a box.

"We can help with the plans. We can list the things we must do. Then we can have pets in class," said Pat.

My cat can hop, too.

This is fun!

Watch my cat skip.

"Not much," said Bob.

"Pets in class will be lots of fun," said Ann.

"I am glad we can make a plan for pets in class!" said Todd.

7

Sam! Sam! You have pep! Look at Sam hop and skip!!

Get that cat!

"Pat's cat hops the best," said Bob.

"You had cats hop and skip in class?" asked Mom.

"What else did the cats do?"

10

The Pet Day

"What did you do in school today?" asked Mom.
"Not much," said Bob.

8

"But today you had pets in class.
Was it fun?" asked Mom. "What did you do?"
"Oh, some stuff," said Bob.

9

Zip and Fudge rushed back to the stump. Their fun ended. But the other animals had a long chuckle!

Open Court Reading

Zip and Fudge

by Carolyn Crimi
illustrated by Kersti Frigell

SRA
A Division of The McGraw-Hill Companies
Columbus, Ohio

2

"You have upset the animals," said the large monster.
"Promise that you will not trick them again!"
"Yes, Yes," muttered Zip and Fudge.

34

Zip and Fudge wanted something to do.
"Let's trick the other animals!" said Zip.

3

Just then, a large monster stepped in front
of Zip and Fudge.
"Did you trick the animals?" thundered the monster.
"Uh . . . uh . . .," stammered Zip and Fudge.

6

They hid until a turtle crept past. "Oh!" yelled Zip and Fudge. The stunned turtle ducked under a rock. "That was fun!" said Zip. "Let's do it again!"

Zip and Fudge scared a bird, a caterpillar, a frog, a giraffe, and a rat. Then Zip said, "This is fun, but I want to rest."

Zip and Fudge curled up in a circle. When they got up, it was dark.

"We'd better run back to the stump," said Zip.

Jill's Biggest Wish

SRA Open Court Reading

by Carlos Molta
illustrated by Kersti Frigell

A Division of *The McGraw-Hill Companies*

Columbus, Ohio

37

The little girl kicked the sand. "Granting wishes just isn't what I want to do," she said. "But I do love to dig!" she said with a wink.

Jill grinned at her new pal. The little girl had granted her biggest and most important wish.

8

"Wish again," said the little girl. "But think of an *important* wish."

"Well," said Jill, "I wish for a pal who will go digging with me."

The little girl tapped her chin. She skipped in a circle, but nothing happened.

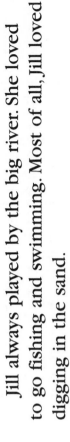

Jill always played by the big river. She loved to go fishing and swimming. Most of all, Jill loved digging in the sand.

"Are you kidding?" gasped Jill.

"Not a bit! Think of a wish!" insisted the little girl.

"Well," said Jill, "I wish for a million dollars."

"In a jiff!" answered the little girl. She tapped her lip and stared at Jill. But nothing happened.

When children visited, Jill said, "You must dig."
The other children were not interested.
One day Jill dug up a little bottle. She patted it
with a rag.

Then, a little girl was in front of Jill.
"Make a wish!" giggled the little girl.

Open Court Reading

Dave the Brave

by Ana Rojas
illustrated by Len Epstein

A Division of *The McGraw-Hill Companies*
Columbus, Ohio

"You're brave, Val," said Dave.
"Yes, Dave," said Val, "But will I ever be
as brave as you?"

8

SRA/McGraw-Hill

A Division of The McGraw-Hill Companies

Copyright © 2000 by SRA/McGraw-Hill.

Printed in the United States of America.

Send all inquiries to:
SRA/McGraw-Hill
8787 Orion Place
Columbus, OH 43240-4027

Just then a big snake came up to Dave and Val.
"I'm afraid of snakes!" said Dave.
"Scram, snake, scram!" yelled Val.
She chased the snake.

"I am the bravest!" Dave said. "Today, I swam across a lake to save a dog."

"But, Dave," said his little sister, Val, "you can't swim."

3

"I raced a truck on a dirt trail," said Dave.

"But, Dave," said Val, "you can't race."

6

4

"I came face-to-face with a big cat in Africa,"
said Dave.
"But, Dave," said Val, "you are scared of cats."

5

"I saved a snake from a dragon," said Dave.
"But, Dave," said Val, "you hate snakes."

45

 **Open Court Reading**

Sleepy Steve

by Peter Matheny
illustrated by Len Epstein

A Division of *The McGraw-Hill Companies*
Columbus, Ohio

Steve climbed up the dinosaur and made a neat nest. "Pleased to meet you," whispered Steve. And the two new pals settled into a deep peaceful sleep.

8

SRA/McGraw-Hill

A Division of The McGraw-Hill Companies

Send all inquiries to:
SRA/McGraw-Hill
8787 Orion Place
Columbus, OH 43240-4027

Then Steve saw a sign near the sticks. "Dinosaurs?" said Steve. "These sticks are a large dinosaur!"

Sleepy Steve was afraid. He hurried into a big building and hid beneath a heap of sticks.

"I am free!" Steve eeked. "But I am very sleepy! I need a place to sleep!"

When Steve was awake, he came from beneath the sticks. He peeked back at them.

"Please tell me what you are," Steve said to the sticks. But the sticks did not speak.

4

Sleepy Steve peeked out from beneath the sticks. "Eeek!" said Steve. He saw big sticks. He saw little sticks. Steve was afraid.

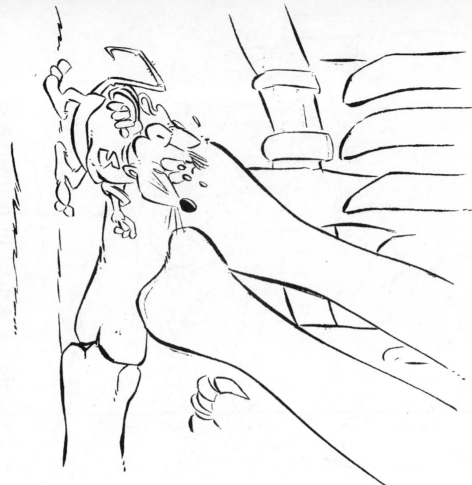

Sleepy Steve began to sneak past the sticks. "Eeek!" said Steve. He saw big feet. He saw little feet. He leaned back and fell asleep where he was.

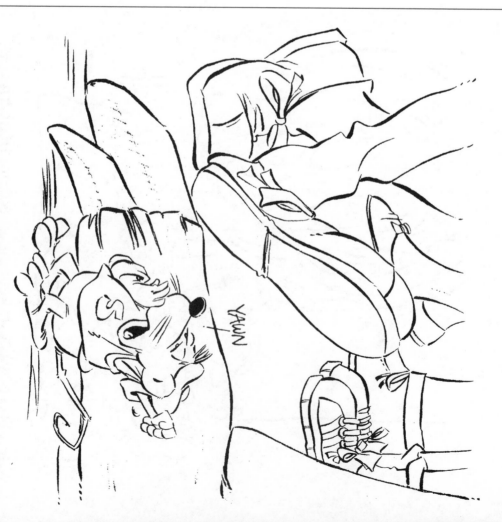

YAWN

SRA Open Court Reading

The Shy Bird's Trick

by Wiley

illustrated by Kersti Frigell

SRA

A Division of The McGraw-Hill Companies

Columbus, Ohio

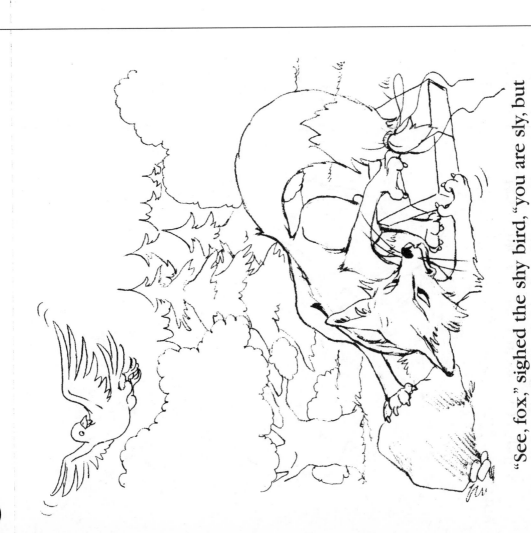

"See, fox," sighed the shy bird, "you are sly, but not as sly as I."

"Bye-bye, sly fox!" cried the bird, and she flew off into the sky.

8

SRA/McGraw-Hill

A Division of The McGraw-Hill Companies

Copyright © 2000 by SRA/McGraw-Hill.

All rights reserved. Except as permitted under the United States
Copyright Act, no part of this publication may be reproduced or
distributed in any form or by any means, or stored in a database
or retrieval system, without prior written permission from the
publisher.

Printed in the United States of America.

Send all inquiries to:
SRA/McGraw-Hill
8787 Orion Place
Columbus, OH 43240-4027

"I will help you," replied the shy bird. "Hold the string
with your long tail while I tie it," she said to the fox.
Then, the shy bird tied the fox's tail to the box in a
tight knot.

"My tail is stuck!" grumbled the fox.

Once a sly fox lived deep in the forest.
The sly fox was very hungry.
"I might die of hunger!" he cried.

3

"Is that a lie?" asked the shy bird.
"Oh, no," cried the sly fox as he licked his lips.
"I need your help."
"I'll bet there is no pie in that box," the shy bird mumbled. "I'll bet that sly fox wants *me* to be the pie!"

6

Then, the sly fox spied a bird flying in the sky.
"I will trick this bird," said the sly fox. "It will make a nice pie."

"Oh, shy little bird," called the sly fox. "You look tired. Come and lie on my soft fur."

The bird in the sky didn't say anything.

"Sweet, shy bird," said the sly fox. "I need your help to tie this string on my pie box. Inside is a yummy pie for my mother."

SRA
**Open Court
Reading**

The Lives of Sea Turtles

by Chris Meramec
illustrated by Diane Blasius

SRA
A Division of The McGraw-Hill Companies
Columbus, Ohio

"Here, little turtle, swim hard," said Carlos. "You have a long way to go. Stay safe. Please come back to our nice beach."

Turtles have lived in the seas for many, many years. Turtles swam in the seas when dinosaurs lived. Those sea turtles were very much like the sea turtles of today.

16

SRA/McGraw-Hill

A Division of *The McGraw-Hill Companies*

Copyright © 2000 by SRA/McGraw-Hill.

All rights reserved. Except as permitted under the United States
Copyright Act, no part of this publication may be reproduced or
distributed in any form or by any means, or stored in a database
or retrieval system, without prior written permission from the
publisher.

Printed in the United States of America.

Send all inquiries to:
SRA/McGraw-Hill
8787 Orion Place
Columbus, OH 43240-4027

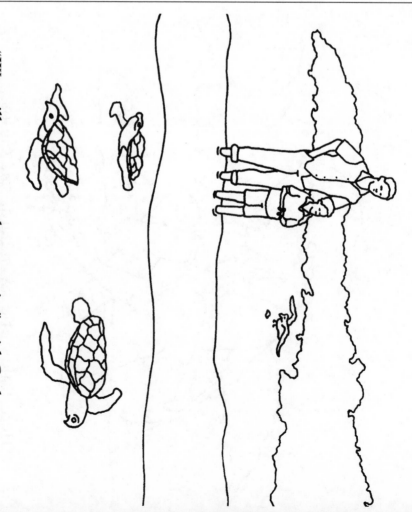

"We will never see them again," said Carlos.
"Yes, you may," said Papa. "Green sea turtles travel
to faraway places like some birds do. But they come
back to the beach where they were born to lay their
eggs. These turtles will come back to this same
beach for as long as they live."

Turtles in the Sea

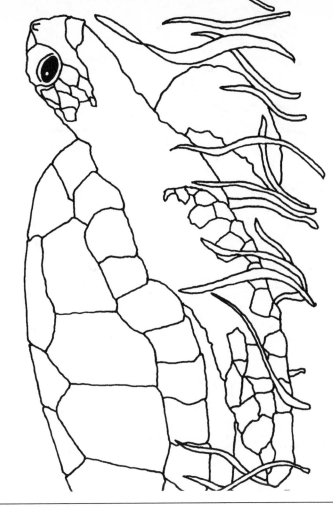

This is a green sea turtle. A sea turtle has flippers for feet. It flaps its flippers like wings when it swims. A sea turtle has a shell that makes swimming easy. The curved top and flat bottom help to lift the shell, and the turtle can glide through the sea.

3

"What will happen to the baby turtles?" asked Carlos.

"When they get to the sea, the little turtles will swim as hard as they can for two days. They will not even stop to eat. They may swim as far as Africa," said Papa.

14

The shell keeps the turtle safe from danger, too. But a sea turtle cannot pull in its head and legs. The sea turtle has a very thick skin and scales on its head and legs.

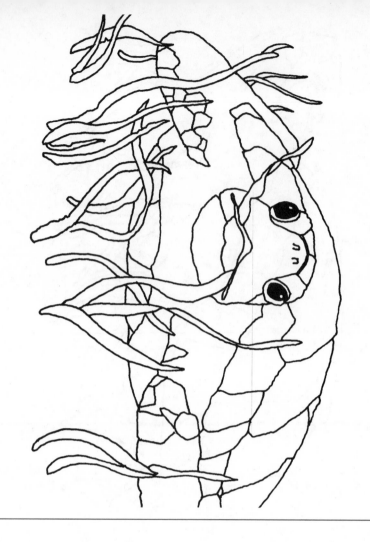

4

"Their little shells are so soft," said Carlos. "Their shells will get harder as the turtles get bigger," said Papa.

"Go away," said Carlos. He waved at the flying gulls.

"Let the little turtles get to the sea!"

"Even then they may not be safe," said Papa. "Big fish eat the soft little turtles, too."

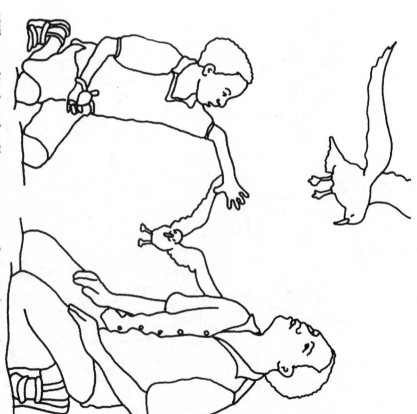

13

Sea turtles eat and sleep in the sea. The green sea turtle eats tender sea grass that lies on the sandy bottom. It swims to the top to breathe.

Turtles do not have teeth, but they do have strong beaks. The beak of a sea turtle can crack shells. Sea turtles might eat shellfish, jellyfish, small sea animals, and wild sea plants.

5

"There are hundreds and hundreds of little turtles!" said Carlos. "See, they are creeping to the sea."

"The little turtles try to get to the sea," said Papa. "But it is a hard trip. Their flippers are made for swimming, not for creeping on land."

12

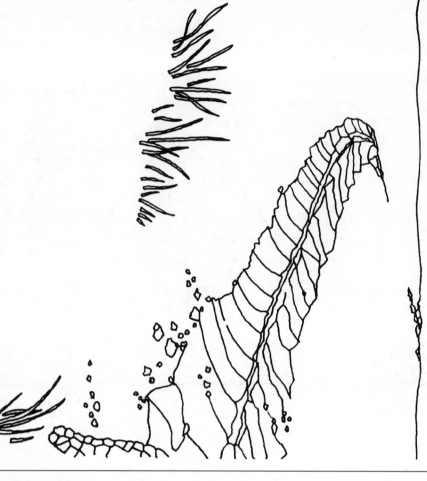

Sea turtles only leave the sea to lay their eggs. A mother turtle digs a nest in the sand. She lays hundreds of eggs in a pile. Then she covers the nest and returns to the sea. The sun keeps the sand and the eggs warm and dry. Mother turtles never see their babies.

6

"Papa!" yelled Carlos. "Come see the birds. They are everywhere on the beach!"

"Turtle eggs must be hatching," said Papa.

"The birds are feasting on baby turtles."

"Baby turtles! Let's hike down there!" said Carlos.

11

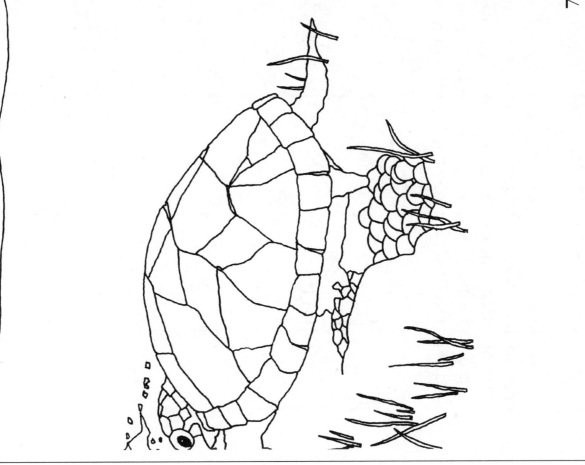

Baby Turtles

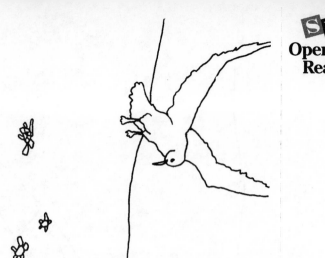

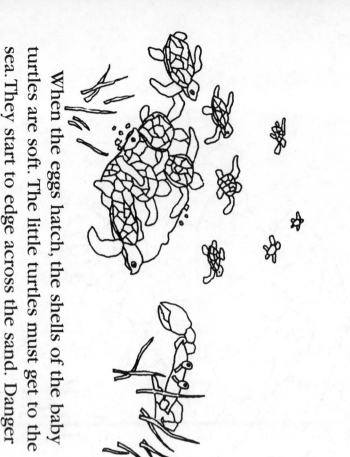

8

When the eggs hatch, the shells of the baby turtles are soft. The little turtles must get to the sea. They start to edge across the sand. Danger awaits. Birds circle high in the sky. They eat many of the little turtles. Crabs eat some, too.

The baby turtles can swim when they are born. They can even find things to eat. But they are still not safe. Big fish hunt the soft little turtles. Hundreds of turtles hatch on the beach. Many will be eaten. Not many will live to be big turtles. At some time they will return to this same beach to lay their eggs.

9

SRA
Open Court Reading

Chinlow of Singboat

by Jo Olson

illustrated by Pat Lucas-Morris

SRA

A Division of *The McGraw-Hill Companies*

Columbus, Ohio

61

Finally, the emperor called Chinlow to him. "Show me," he said. Chinlow looked into the face of a tiny rose. The rose grew and became lovely. Then the emperor said to Chinlow, "Now look at me."

Chinlow looked into the emperor's eyes. The emperor saw love in her eyes. "Now I know her talent," he said, "and I am not afraid of it. Her talent is love."

8

SRA/McGraw-Hill

A Division of The McGraw-Hill Companies

Copyright © 2000 by SRA/McGraw-Hill.

All rights reserved. Except as permitted under the United States Copyright Act, no part of this publication may be reproduced or distributed in any form or by any means, or stored in a database or retrieval system, without prior written permission from the publisher.

Printed in the United States of America.

Send all inquiries to:
SRA/McGraw-Hill
8787 Orion Place
Columbus, OH 43240-4027

2

Chinlow looked into the face of a tiny rose. The rose Chinlow looked at began to grow until it became the loveliest rose in the garden.

Each teacher said, "I saw her talent, but I do not know it."

7

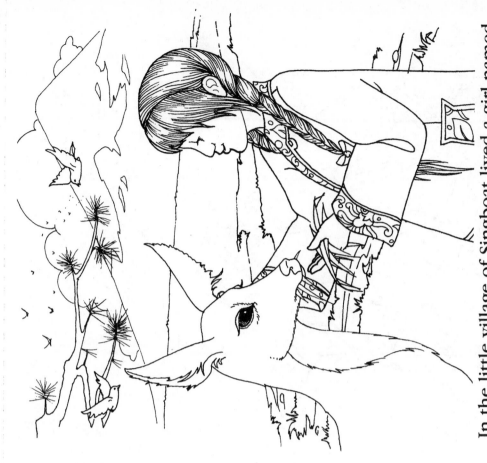

In the little village of Singboat lived a girl named Chinlow. She loved nature. Nature loved her. The birds of the forest sang more sweetly for her. The doe of the forest ate from her hand. The snows on the hills shone whitest for her.

3

The emperor called for his wisest teachers. "I must know," he said, "the talent of Chinlow." One by one the teachers spoke to Chinlow. "Show me," each teacher said.

6

The roses Chinlow planted would always grow tall. "Where does Chinlow's talent come from?" people of the village asked. "Even the rainbow is more dazzling over Chinlow's home."

4

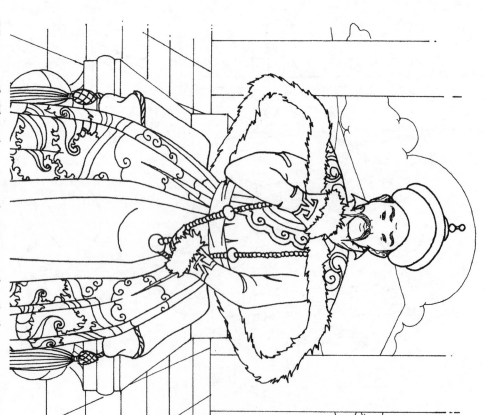

News of Chinlow's talent reached the emperor in faraway Pancoat.

"Could the talent of a simple child overthrow the emperor?" he wondered. "I must not let this go on."

5

Mrs. Music

SRA Open Court Reading

by Carolyn Crimi
illustrated by Anthony Accardo

A Division of The McGraw-Hill Companies

Columbus, Ohio

The next day Mrs. Music and Stu went for their walk.
"Oh, my!" said Mrs. Music when she saw the bugle.
"Stu, look at that beautiful bugle! I wonder where
I can put it?"

8

2

SRA/McGraw-Hill
A Division of The McGraw-Hill Companies

Copyright © 2000 by SRA/McGraw-Hill.

All rights reserved. Except as permitted under the United States Copyright Act, no part of this publication may be reproduced or distributed in any form or by any means, or stored in a database or retrieval system, without prior written permission from the publisher.

Printed in the United States of America.

Send all inquiries to:
SRA/McGraw-Hill
8787 Orion Place
Columbus, OH 43240-4027

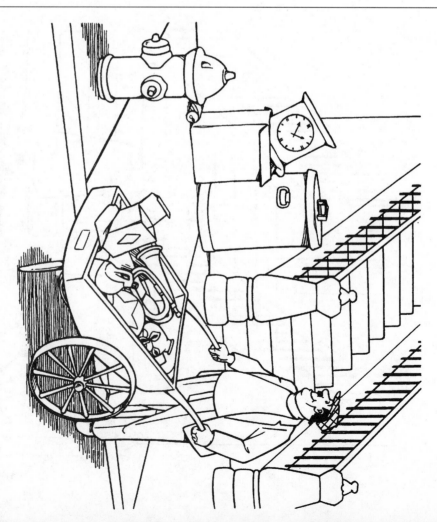

Later that day Mr. Quinlan came by with his cart. "What a beautiful clock!" he cried. "It must be valuable. I will take it home."

But Mr. Quinlan's cart was full. "A cleaning is needed," Mr. Quinlan said. "I don't use this bugle anymore. I will throw it away."

7

Open Court
Reading

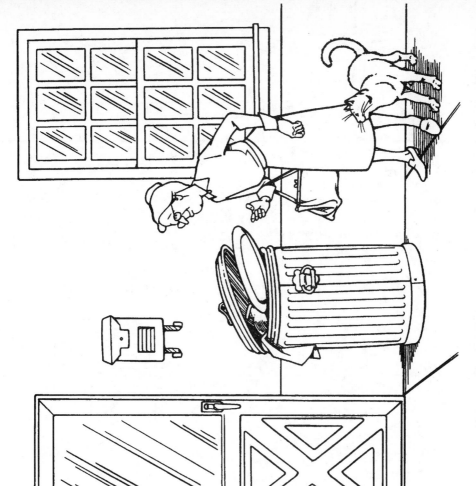

Every day Mrs. Music and her cat Stu went for a stroll. "Look!" Mrs. Music said one day to Stu. "Someone has thrown a beautiful dish into the trash! That dish would look grand on my table."

3

Hugo put the candlesticks on Aunt Iris's shelf. The candlesticks were beautiful, but the shelf was full. "Hugo," said Aunt Iris, "a cleaning is needed! I don't use this clock anymore. I have quite a few others. I will throw this one away."

6

67

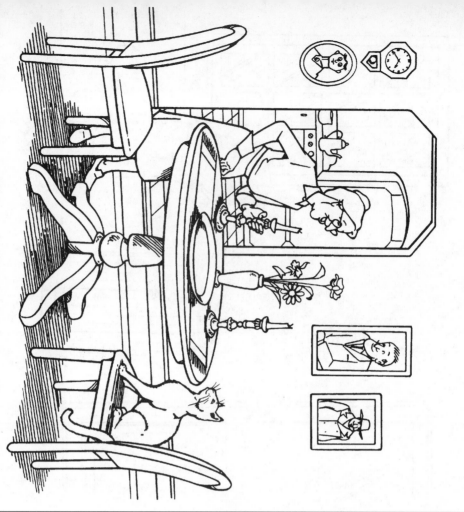

Mrs. Music rushed home and put the dish on her table. The dish was beautiful, but the table was full.

"Stu," said Mrs. Music, "a cleaning is needed! I don't use these candlesticks anymore. I will throw them away."

4

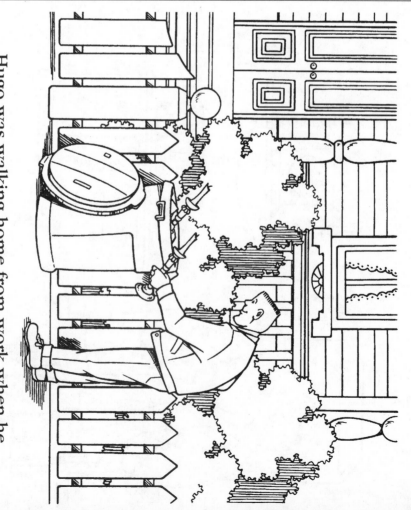

Hugo was walking home from work when he saw the candlesticks.

"What unusual candlesticks!" he said to himself. "They must have come from a museum. Aunt Iris would love them!"

Hugo picked up the candlesticks and took them to his aunt.

5

SRA Open Court Reading

Root Stew

by Marie Foster
illustrated by Deborah Colvin Borgo

A Division of The McGraw-Hill Companies
Columbus, Ohio

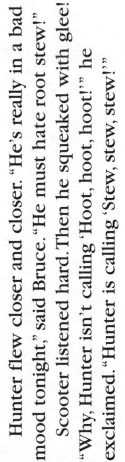

Hunter flew closer and closer. "He's really in a bad
mood tonight," said Bruce. "He must hate root stew!"
Scooter listened hard. Then he squeaked with glee!
"Why, Hunter isn't calling 'Hoot, hoot, hoot!'" he
exclaimed. "Hunter is calling 'Stew, stew, stew!'"

8

SRA/McGraw-Hill

A Division of The McGraw-Hill Companies

Copyright © 2000 by SRA/McGraw-Hill.

All rights reserved. Except as permitted under the United States Copyright Act, no part of this publication may be reproduced or distributed in any form or by any means, or stored in a database or retrieval system, without prior written permission from the publisher.

Printed in the United States of America.

Send all inquiries to:
SRA/McGraw-Hill
8787 Orion Place
Columbus, OH 43240-4027

2

As the moon rose, Scooter and Bruce listened. In the distance, they heard Hunter's call. "Hoot, hoot, hoot! Hoot, hoot, hoot!"

"Rats!" said Scooter gloomily. "He didn't like the root stew."

7

70

71

The next day, Scooter worked. Into a pot he tossed chopped roots, berries, and shoots. That night, before the moon rose, Scooter crept over to Hunter's roost. There, he left the pot of root stew.

6

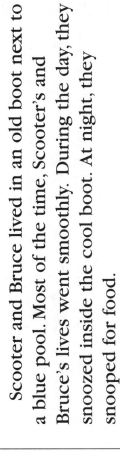

Scooter and Bruce lived in an old boot next to a blue pool. Most of the time, Scooter's and Bruce's lives went smoothly. During the day, they snoozed inside the cool boot. At night, they snooped for food.

3

The only time Scooter's and Bruce's lives did not go smoothly was when the moon was bright. When the moon was bright, they hid in the boot and listened for Hunter's "Hoot, hoot, hoot."

They knew that "Hoot, hoot, hoot" meant that Hunter was hungry. Mice were not safe when Hunter was hungry.

4

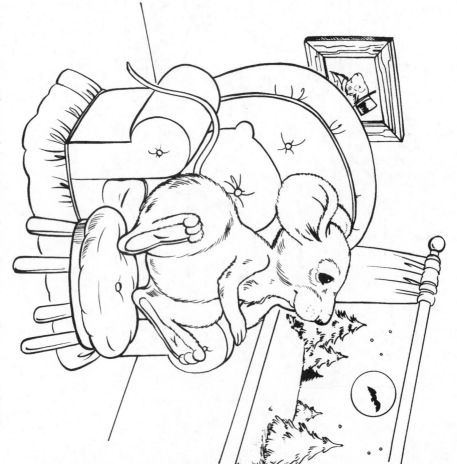

Scooter thought it was his duty to do something about Hunter.

"Hunter always seems hungry," he said, "and he always seems to be in a bad mood. Maybe Hunter isn't getting anything nice to eat."

5

Open Court Reading

A Day in the Amazon

by Dottie Raymer
illustrated by Pat Lucas-Morris

A Division of The McGraw-Hill Companies

Columbus, Ohio

In the trees above, only the three-toed sloth remains quiet. It moves so slowly that mold grows on its fur. The green mold helps it hide in the leaves.

The sloth isn't moving at all. The lazy sloth is asleep. When night comes, it will slowly wake to eat.

8

SRA/McGraw-Hill

A Division of The McGraw-Hill Companies

Printed in the United States of America.

Send all inquiries to:
SRA/McGraw-Hill
8787 Orion Place
Columbus, OH 43240-4027

2

A jaguar slips silently through the trees below. The jaguar's spotted coat hides it well. It stops beside a stream and dips its tail into the water. A fish rises to the bait. Surprise! The jaguar has a tasty meal.

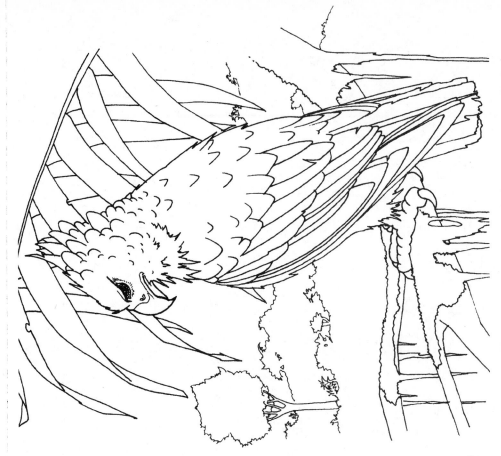

It is a peaceful day in the Amazon. A light breeze shakes the tree leaves.

High above the jungle, a huge eagle watches as the rain forest wakes up. So far, the day seems still.

3

Nearby, a giant anteater opens an ant nest. It pokes its long nose into the nest to find its tiny food.

6

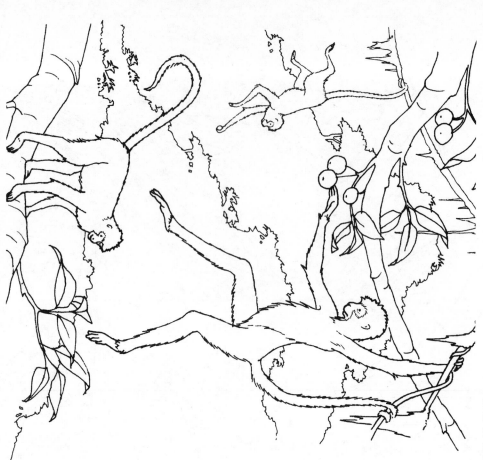

But the rain forest is never completely quiet. Deep in the jungle, creatures stir. Spider monkeys leap from tree to tree. Their tails grab long vines as they find their way to ripe fruit.

4

A bird perches in a fig tree. It uses its bright beak to snip off a fig. It throws the fig into the air. It catches the fig in its beak.

5

Open Court Reading

Hugo Bugle

by Dennis Fertig
illustrated by Robert Byrd

A Division of The McGraw-Hill Companies

Columbus, Ohio

"So, Joan, will you try it?" asked Hugo.
"No, thanks," said Joan. "I will simply use my phone."

16

2

"No matter where you go on the globe, you can easily use the unit. If you tie it on your chin, you can use it when you ride a bike, row a boat, or fly in a plane."

15

Toast

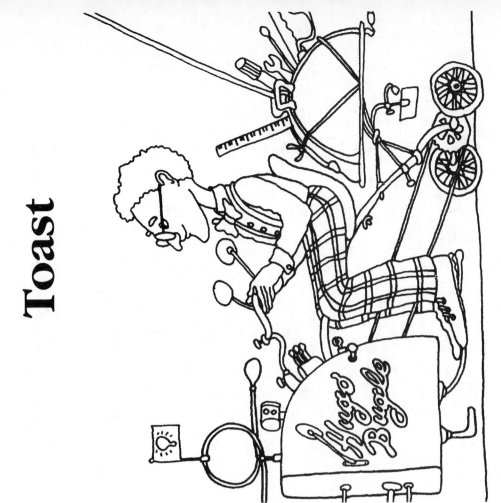

"Spike, I have a new idea," said Hugo. "It is a faster way to have toast when you wake up."

3

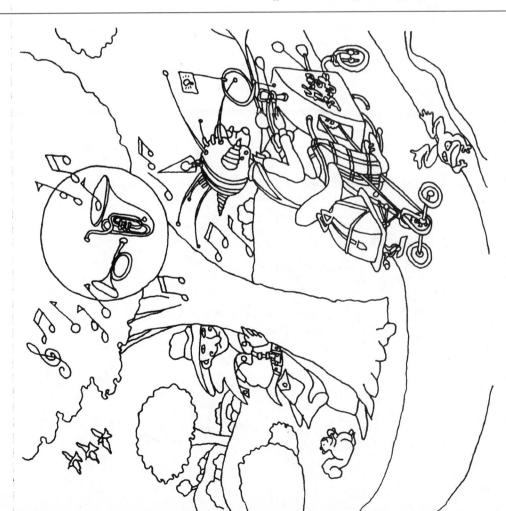

"The code is made of blaring tones from bugle, flute, and tuba music. A spy will not have a clue to what you say. A spy will hear the happiest tune, not a clue."

14

"At night, tie a shiny pie plate to a wire. Make the wire go to a window. Set a bag of marbles by the window. By the bed, put a few stones."

4

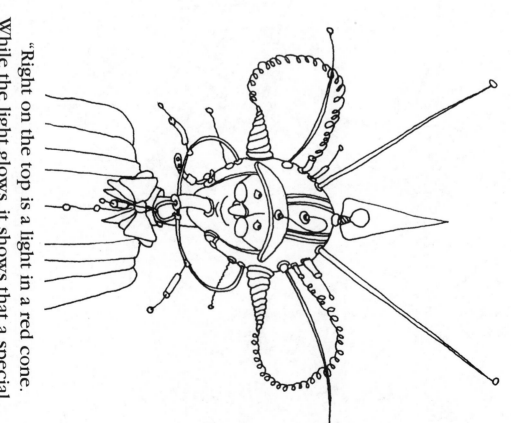

"Right on the top is a light in a red cone. While the light glows, it shows that a special microchip is in use. The microchip changes speech into code."

13

Open Court Reading

"Place a tube on the side of the window. Below the tube, glue the blue pail to the end of a pole. Put the pole under the lower window."

5

81

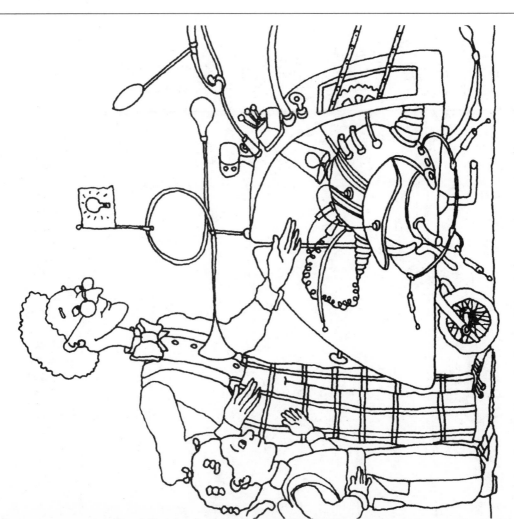

"The unit is a huge hat. It has wires, fuses, and tubes. Use the blue tube to speak. To hear, use the white tubes in the holes on the sides."

12

6

"Tie a rope to this side of the window. Tie a heavy ice cube tray to the rope. Use the heaviest one you can find. Load the toaster. Go to bed."

A New Unit

"Joan, you might like my new idea," said Hugo.
"I will try," said Joan with a shining smile.
"It is a unit that you use to speak to any human, even miles away," said Hugo.

11

"Wake up to noisy music. Scoop some of the heavier stones into the shiny pie plate. When the shiny plate drops, the window opens."

7

"Tell me the truth, Spike. Is this a cool idea?" asked Hugo.

"Oh, my. The idea is nice," said Spike. "But I do not like toast."

10

8

"When the top window opens, sliding marbles go through the tube. The pail fills, and the pole dives low. Then the lower window pops wide open."

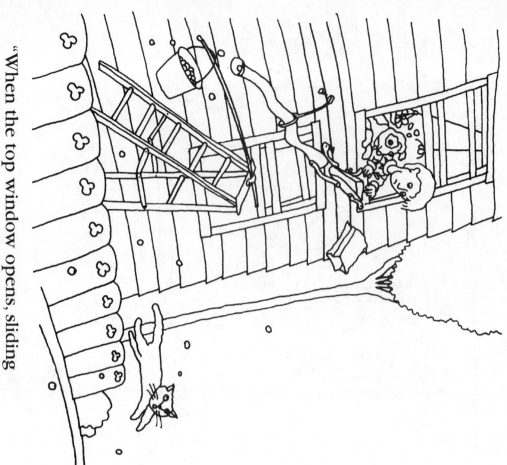

"The heavy ice cube tray hits the right spot. And very soon, up pop the warmest slices of toast."

9

Open Court
Reading

Fran's Gift

by Carolyn Crimi
illustrated by Anthony Accardo

SRA

A Division of The McGraw-Hill Companies

Columbus, Ohio

Then Fran gave the queen her scarf.
"This scarf," said the queen, "will keep me warm,
and green and blue stripes are charming! You will be
a smart queen, Fran."
And Fran was.

8

SRA/McGraw-Hill

A Division of The McGraw-Hill Companies

Copyright © 2000 by SRA/McGraw-Hill.

Printed in the United States of America.

Send all inquiries to:
SRA/McGraw-Hill
8787 Orion Place
Columbus, OH 43240-4027

2

The next day, the girls took their gifts to the queen.

"Here is a sparkling cart," said Martha. "See how it shines!"

"This marble throne is the largest in the kingdom!" said Greta.

"These gifts are very charming," said the queen, "but I already have a cart and a throne."

7

86

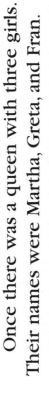

Once there was a queen with three girls. Their names were Martha, Greta, and Fran.

"Tomorrow is my birthday," said the queen to the girls. "The girl who finds the smartest and most useful gift will be the next queen."

3

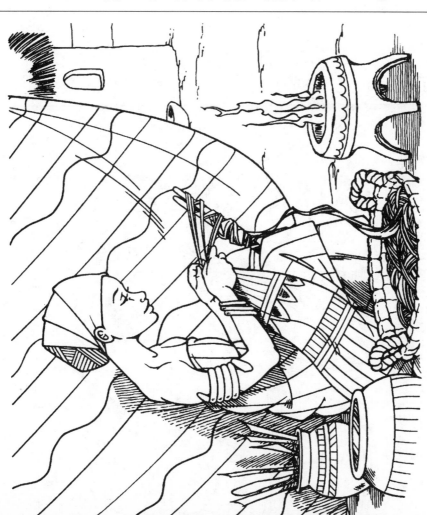

Fran knit and knit. By twilight, her arms hurt, but the scarf still wasn't finished.

"I will work into the night," she said.

Martha and Greta sneered. "Think of missing a grand party for a silly scarf."

6

Martha and Greta worried. "There is a grand party tonight!" they said. "We must get a gift quickly or we will miss the party!"

"The market is close," said Martha. "I will run there and purchase Mother a sparkling cart."

"Martha is smart," thought Greta. "I will run to the market, too. I will buy Mother a marble throne."

4

The youngest girl, Fran, puzzled over her mother's gift. Finally, she said, "I will knit a scarf with stripes." Fran bought yards of green and blue yarn and started to work.

Fran's sisters spoke shrilly to her. "Our gifts are more charming," they said. "You will have to work hard. You will miss the grand party!"

5

SRA Open Court Reading

A Book for Mr. Hook

by Carolyn Crimi
illustrated by Kersti Frigell

SRA

A Division of *The McGraw-Hill Companies*
Columbus, Ohio

Lucy read her book to Mr. Hook every day. One day, the children came to play at the brook. "Why doesn't Mr. Hook yell at us anymore?" they asked Lucy's mother.

"He's got a new friend," she said.

"Who?" the children asked.

"Peter Pan," said Lucy's mother.

8

SRA/McGraw-Hill

A Division of The McGraw-Hill Companies

Copyright © 2000 by SRA/McGraw-Hill.

Printed in the United States of America.

Send all inquiries to:
SRA/McGraw-Hill
8787 Orion Place
Columbus, OH 43240-4027

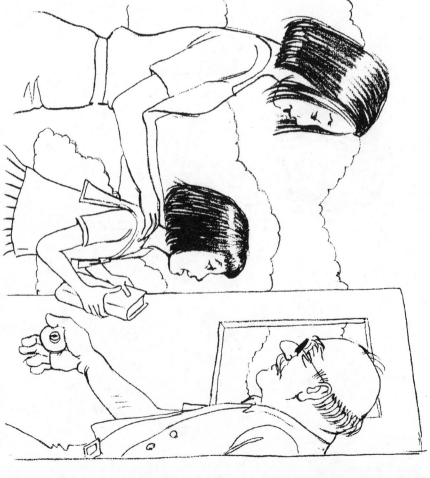

Lucy and her mother took the book to Mr. Hook's house. "My teacher said I need to practice reading. May I read my book to you?"

"What book?" yelled Mr. Hook.

"*Peter Pan,*" said Lucy.

"Hmm," said Mr. Hook. "Well, okay…"

91

Once an old man named Mr. Hook lived by a brook in the woods. Whenever the children played by the brook, the old man yelled, "Stay away from my brook!"

3

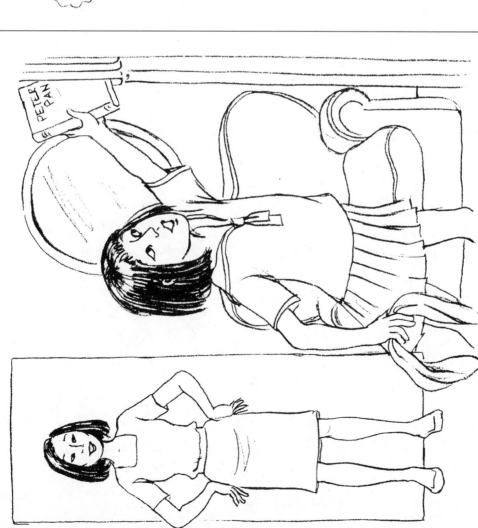

Lucy took off the cloth. She went to her bookshelf and chose a book. "This is a good book," she said. "I'll bet Mr. Hook would like it."

Lucy's mother understood. "Good idea!" she said.

6

4

"Why does he act like that?" Lucy asked her mother. Lucy's mother said that Mr. Hook was blind. She took a cloth and tied it across Lucy's eyes. "Here," she said. "Maybe this will help you understand how Mr. Hook feels."

5

Lucy tried putting on her shoes. She could not even find her foot.

Worst of all, Lucy could not read. "I don't know what I would do if I could not read books!" said Lucy.

Open Court Reading

Taffy for Uncle Warren

by Marie Foster
illustrated by Gary Undercuffler

A Division of The McGraw-Hill Companies

Columbus, Ohio

93

Uncle Warren tossed the hook and taffy into the water. Suddenly, a fish jumped up and grabbed the hook.

"I've got one! I've got one!" yelled Uncle Warren.

"At last!"

Marcella grinned at her smiling uncle. "Yes!" she said.

"A good piece of taffy can do anything!"

8

2

Every day after that, Marcella returned to the pier to give taffy to her uncle.

One day, during a really delightful story, Marcella dropped a piece of taffy into the water. A fish snatched the taffy and quickly swam away. Uncle Warren stared at the fish. Then he stuck a piece of taffy onto his fishhook.

7

Open Court Reading

Uncle Warren was an unhappy man. Every day, he went to the end of the pier to fish. Uncle Warren never got anything. He just sat lonely and unhappy. Everyone thought he was just disagreeable.

3

"Remember my first piece of taffy?" she asked. "I had a useless tooth that wouldn't come out. You said a good piece of taffy would get my tooth out. You said a good piece of taffy could do anything."

The story made Uncle Warren grin. Marcella hadn't seen him grin in a very long time.

6

Uncle Warren's niece, Marcella, was an unselfish girl. She worried about him. Every day, she watched him on the pier. One chilly, rainy morning Marcella made a decision. She went to the end of the pier.

"Look what I have, Uncle Warren! Taffy! Your favorite candy!" she called. Uncle Warren didn't say anything.

4

"Have some, Uncle. It tastes wonderful!" said Marcella. Before Uncle Warren could disagree, Marcella popped a piece of the taffy into his mouth. Uncle Warren silently chewed the taffy.

As her uncle ate, Marcella retold a funny story.

5

Open Court
Reading

The Prince's Foolish Wish

by Laura Edwards
illustrated by Linda Kelen

A Division of The McGraw-Hill Companies
Columbus, Ohio

"Arf, Arf," said Pooch.

Drip, drip, splash, splash went the water.

"Let's eat!" said Walter. And he didn't worry over his silver ever again.

16

This time Walter was careful. He stopped to think. Then he said, "I wish that everything would return to the way it was."

"Commendable. Your wish is granted," said the worm.

The Prince and the Worm

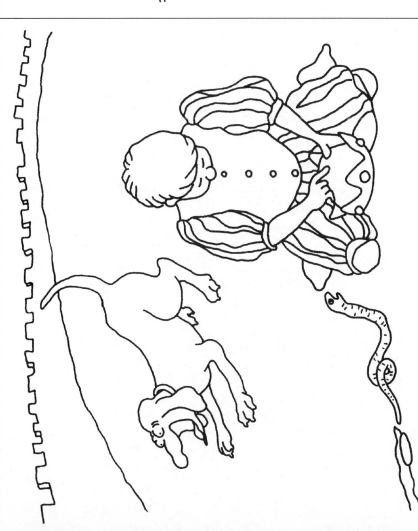

Walter was a selfish prince. He liked only two things. He liked his dog Pooch, and he liked silver. He had piles and piles of silver. Each night he would lock his treasure room. Each morning he would unlock his treasure room. Then he would stack and restack the piles of silver.

"Oh, worm, you were right. I made a foolish wish. I can't eat. I turned poor Pooch to silver. I want to eat. I want Pooch to be furry again. I want to return to the way I was."

"You have just one more wish," said the worm. "Do you want to eat? Do you want Pooch back? Try to be wise. Do not make an unwise wish."

One day Walter was playing with Pooch in the garden. The sunlight sparkled on the water in the pool. This made Walter wonder, "Wouldn't it be wonderful if the pool were filled with silver?"

All of a sudden, Walter heard a splash. He spotted a little worm in the water. He lifted the worm from the pool. Walter was ready to toss the worm away. Suddenly it spoke.

4

"Pooch! Poor Pooch! Worm! Worm! I need you!" cried Walter.

The little worm poked its head out of the earth. "How can a worthless worm help a wealthy prince?" asked the worm.

13

Walter returned to the garden. Pooch had a bone. "Look, Pooch," said Walter. "We can play with a silver bone."

Walter picked up the bone. It turned to silver.

He tossed the bone across the path. Pooch fetched the bone and returned to Walter.

"Nice dog, Pooch," said Walter. He bent over to pet Pooch on the head. In an instant, Pooch froze. Instantly, Pooch turned to silver!

12

101

"Don't throw me away," said the worm.

"Why not?" asked Walter. "What is a little worm worth to me?"

The worm said, "I am not worthless. I'm a magic worm. I can grant you three wishes. What do you want?"

"I would like my pool filled with silver," said Walter.

5

"So it is," said the worm.
When the pool filled with silver, Walter was unable to speak. "I am speechless," he said to the worm.

"You have two more wishes," said the worm.

"But I must warn you to take care. Be careful what you wish."

Walter heard only the words *two more wishes*. The worm's warning was unheard. Walter quickly made a second wish.

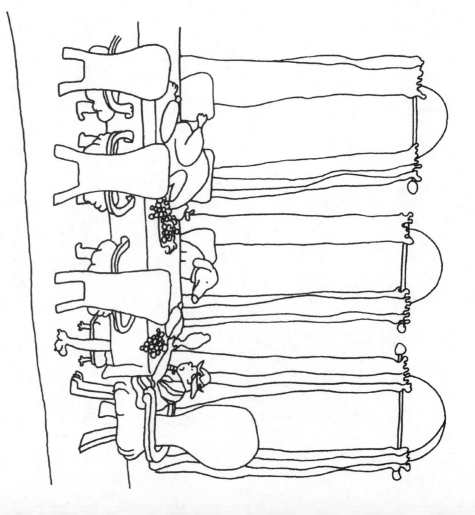

But Walter soon discovered his first problem. Each bite he tried to eat turned to silver. He was unable to eat anything. Soon he had a plate of uneaten silver food. He felt much discomfort.

"I wish that everything I touch would turn to silver," said Walter.

"That is not a wise wish," said the worm.

"Your job is to grant my wish," said Walter. "You heard what I want."

"Your wish is granted," said the worm. "Perhaps you will learn a lesson. Only a fool makes foolish wishes."

The Foolish Wish

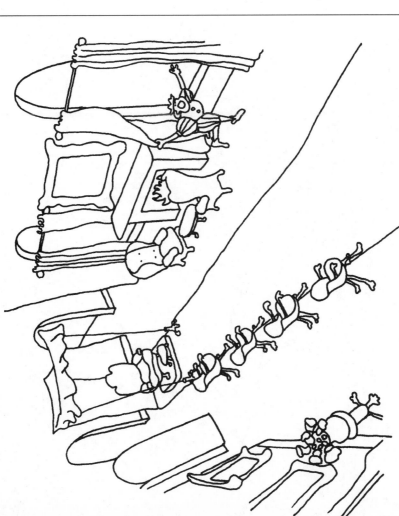

Walter rushed into his palace. He put his hand on each thing he spied. Soon he had silver carpets, silver tables, and a silver throne.

"I'm hungry," said Walter. "I will have lunch, then I will spend all afternoon turning things to silver."

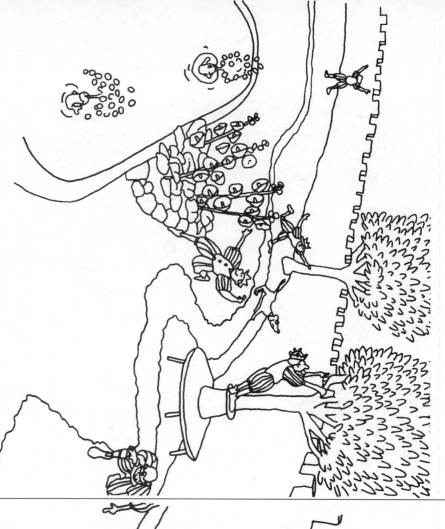

Walter ran through the garden. He touched chairs, the roses, and the stones on the path. Everything turned to silver.

"It works! It works!" cried Walter. "Watch this!" He put his hand under the water. Clink, clink, clink! He heard the silver drip into a pile.

"Yes, it works," said the worm. "I will dig into the soft earth. That is where I will be when you need me."

"I won't need you," snapped Walter. "I have all the wealth I need. A wealthy prince does not need a worthless little worm."

8

9

Open Court Reading

Flower the Cow

by Dottie Raymer

illustrated by Deborah Colvin Borgo

SRA

A Division of The McGraw-Hill Companies

Columbus, Ohio

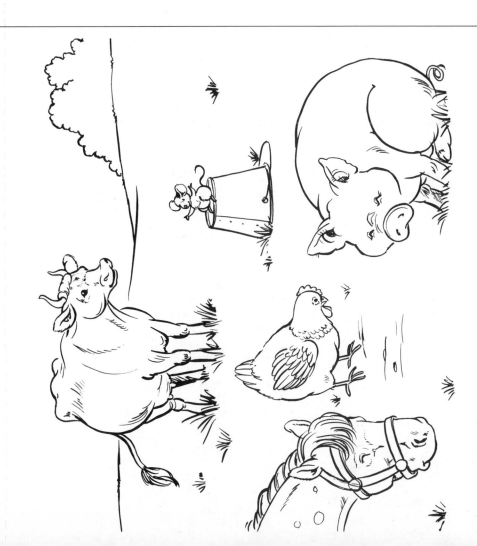

Scooter looked around at the animals. They looked down at the ground.

"It sounds," said the mouse, "like some animals around here a re too proud...but I doubt that Flower is one of them!"

8

Finally, little Scooter the mouse spoke up. "Well, I don't know about plowing, or rooting, or laying eggs," she said.

"But I do know that you can always count on Flower for just the right amount of sweet milk."

Once a brown cow named Flower lived on a farm just outside of town.

Flower stayed mostly out in the field. She kept her head down, and never seemed to notice the other animals around the farm.

3

107

"Root around?" clucked the hens and other barnyard fowl. "That's nothing to be proud of. However, if she could lay eggs like ours, now that would be something to be proud of!"

6

4

"How can that cow be so proud?" Howdy the horse wondered aloud. "Why, she can't even pull a plow!"

"Pull a plow?" shouted Stout the sow. "That's nothing to be proud of! However, if she could root around in the ground with her snout, now that would be something to be proud of!"

5

Open Court Reading

Paul, Aunt Maud, and Claude

by Carolyn Crimi
illustrated by Kersti Frigell

A Division of The McGraw-Hill Companies

Columbus, Ohio

"You found him!" said Aunt Maud happily.
"You returned my pet tiger!"
Aunt Maud gave the exhausted Claude a kiss. Then she turned to Paul. "Now can you help me find my pet lion?"

8

SRA/McGraw-Hill

A Division of The McGraw-Hill Companies

Copyright © 2000 by SRA/McGraw-Hill.

Printed in the United States of America.

Send all inquiries to:
SRA/McGraw-Hill
8787 Orion Place
Columbus, OH 43240-4027

2

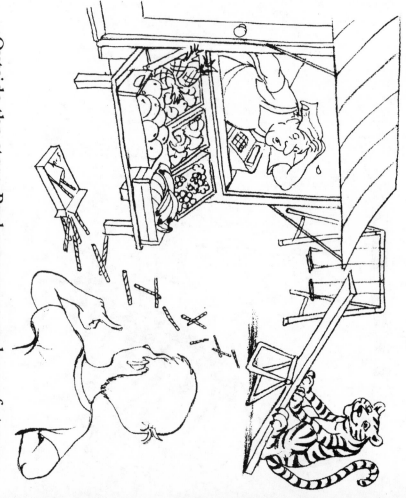

Outside the store, Paul saw an open box of straws. "Claude must have been here, too!" said Paul. He followed the straws until he came to the playground. There sat Claude on the seesaw.

"You must be hungry, Claude," said Paul cautiously. Paul gave Claude some sausage. Then, with a trail of raw cauliflower, he slowly led the tiger back home.

7

Paul's Aunt Maud owned a tiger named Claude.
Claude had four big paws with sharp claws.
"Claude is really quite tame," said Aunt Maud.
"I have even taught him tricks."

3

One day Aunt Maud looked distraught.
"Claude must be lost!" she said.
"I can help," said Paul.
Paul ran across Maud's lawn to a dairy farm.
"These cows look awfully scared," thought Paul.
"I'll bet Claude has been here."
He looked down and saw buttermilk paw
prints. He followed them to a nearby store.

6

Paul watched as Claude performed his tricks. Claude could turn somersaults. He could balance on a seesaw. He could even do laundry!

"He must be an awfully smart tiger," thought Paul.

4

"How do you get Claude to do these tricks?" asked Paul.

"I feed him well," said Aunt Maud. "He likes to gnaw on sausages and raw cauliflower, and he loves to sip buttermilk through a straw."

5

SRA Open Court Reading

Toy Store Explorer

by Zena Smith
illustrated by Deborah Colvin Borgo

SRA

A Division of The McGraw-Hill Companies

Columbus, Ohio

Well, here is my choice. It's a bright plastic coil that does all kinds of tricks.

8

SRA/McGraw-Hill

A Division of The McGraw-Hill Companies

Copyright © 2000 by SRA/McGraw-Hill.

Printed in the United States of America.

Send all inquiries to:
SRA/McGraw-Hill
8787 Orion Place
Columbus, OH 43240-4027

There's still so much more to see. There are games, books, jigsaw puzzles, and so many more toys. What can I choose?

Open Court
Reading

115

There are shelves of dolls. They come in all
shapes and sizes. Here's a princess in a royal gown.
Another doll has a voice that sounds almost human.

6

I like to explore Roy's wonderful toy store.
Here's a shiny kite made completely of red,
green, yellow, and blue foil. What a spectacular
sight that would be in the sky.

3

Now here's another fine choice. It's a model of a ship. It's a destroyer. Look at all the pieces. I'd need glue to join them all.

Next is an oil truck with a cab and trailer. They come apart. It also has a flexible hose.

117

SRA
Open Court
Reading

Rock Collecting

by Carolyn Crimi
illustrated by Gary Undercuffler

SRA

A Division of The McGraw-Hill Companies

Columbus, Ohio

So the next time you are walking, you might just find the rock that will make you a rock collector well into the future!

8

SRA/McGraw-Hill

A Division of The McGraw-Hill Companies

Printed in the United States of America.

Send all inquiries to:
SRA/McGraw-Hill
8787 Orion Place
Columbus, OH 43240-4027

Rocks are not just for studying. Small rocks can be painted with smiling faces or made to look like tiny mice. Two large rocks might make a nice set of bookends. A giant rock might be just the right size for climbing.

Rocks with fossils are highly prized by serious collectors. These rocks contain the remains or marks from plants and animals that were alive long ago. Fossils turn up in the most surprising places. Keep your eyes open. You might find one, too!

Have you ever picked up a rock out of the soil just because you liked the way it looked?

If you like looking at rocks, you might become a rock collector. Rock collectors are people who are curious about rocks.

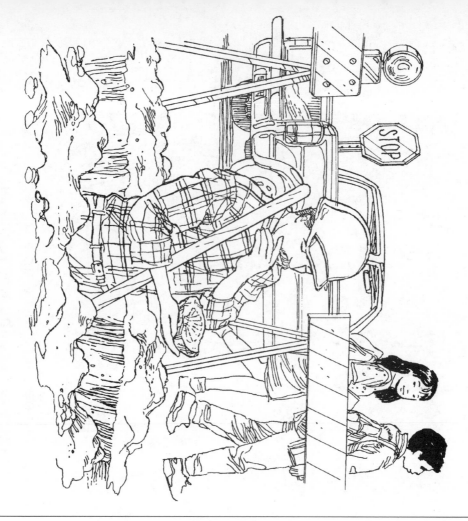

Rocks are a part of nature. You might find rocks by rivers. You might find them on the beach. You might even find them along a street in a town.

4

Different kinds of rocks have different features. Some rocks, like limestone, are quite soft. These rocks easily break into powder. Others, like quartzite, are hard.

Quartz

Granite

Moon Rock

Slate

Limestone

Basalt

5

Open Court Reading

Joyce Writes a Good Story

by Carolyn Crimi
illustrated by Meg McLean

A Division of The McGraw-Hill Companies
Columbus, Ohio

"Your story was really good!" said Soo Lin.

"So was yours!" said Joyce. "We don't ever have to be afraid again . . . as long as we are in the same room and can help each other feel brave."

16

SRA/McGraw-Hill

A Division of The McGraw-Hill Companies

Copyright © 2000 by SRA/McGraw-Hill.

All rights reserved. Except as permitted under the United States Copyright Act, no part of this publication may be reproduced or distributed in any form or by any means, or stored in a database or retrieval system, without prior written permission from the publisher.

Printed in the United States of America.

Send all inquiries to:
SRA/McGraw-Hill
8787 Orion Place
Columbus, OH 43240-4027

2

When Joyce stood up to read, her knees shook. She felt awful. She felt awkward. Then she looked at Soo Lin, who was smiling. Joyce felt better. She read her story, and the class applauded.

15

123

A Good Idea

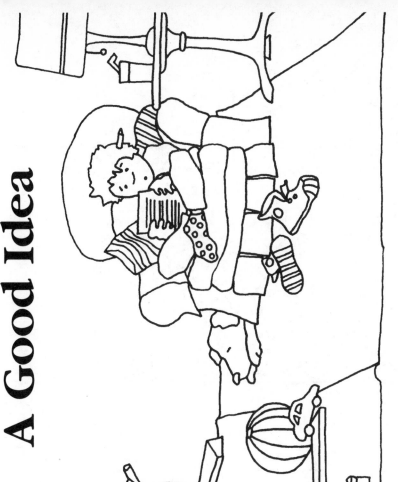

Joyce had to write a story for school. She thought and thought, but she did not know what to write about.

"Why not write about a boy and his toys," said her brother.

Joyce did not want to write about a boy and his toys.

3

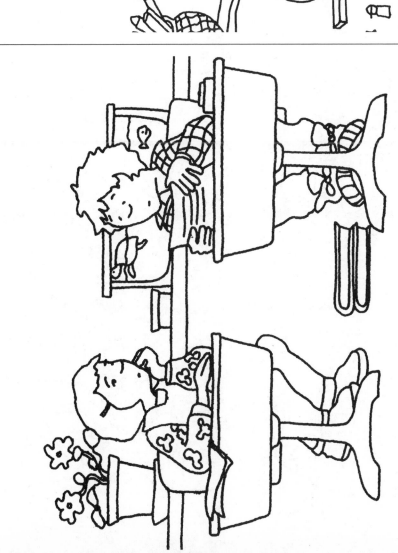

At school, Joyce talked to her friend Soo Lin. "I'm afraid to read my story out loud," she said to Soo Lin.

"Me, too!" said Soo Lin. "But I thought I was the only one who was afraid."

"I know!" Soo Lin went on. "I'll look at you, and you look at me when we read. Maybe that will help us feel brave."

14

4

Joyce's sister said, "Why not write about a girl with brown hair and a beautiful voice?"

"That would not be my first choice," said Joyce.

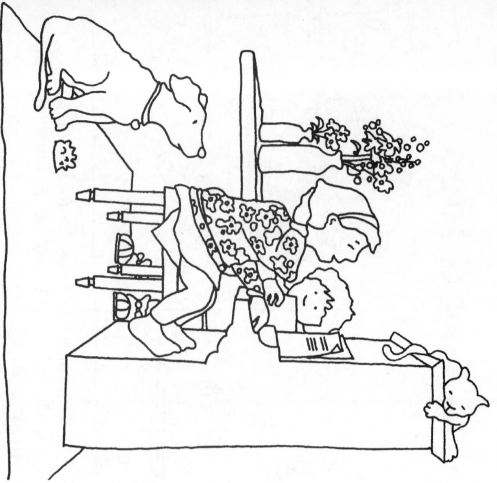

Joyce caught the school bus. She saw Howard and Shawn.

"We know our stories by heart," said Shawn.

Joyce felt worse. She wanted to know her story by heart, too. She tried to practice reading it on the bus, but the boys and girls were too noisy.

13

124

125

Joyce's father was in the garden watering flowers. Joyce asked him what she should write about.

"You could write about a man and his flowers," said her father.

"No," said Joyce. "That's not good."

5

Joyce looked for her books. She took her time. She did not care if she was late. She wished she could avoid school today.

12

Next door, Joyce saw Howard and Shawn playing football on the lawn.

"Have you finished your story?" asked Shawn.

"Not yet," said Joyce.

"You should do it now," said Howard. "We must read them out loud tomorrow."

6

Joyce in Class

"I am afraid to read my story out loud to the class," said Joyce.

"Calm down," said Mom. "The class will enjoy your story. But hurry or you will be late for school!"

11

127

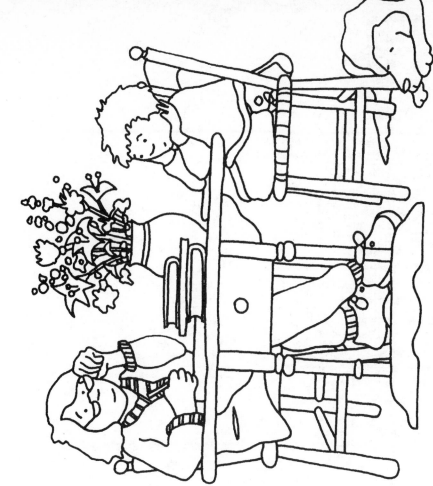

Joyce took out her notebook. Her sister entered the room.

"What is your story about?" asked her sister.

"A girl who does not know what to write about," said Joyce.

"Am I in your story?" asked her sister.

"Of course!" said Joyce.

Joyce found Mom and sat down with a frown.

"Did you think of something to write about?" asked Mom.

Joyce shook her head.

"You should write about the things you know best," said Mom.

7

Joyce went for a walk. She walked and talked to herself. She thought about what her mother had said. Suddenly, Joyce had an idea.

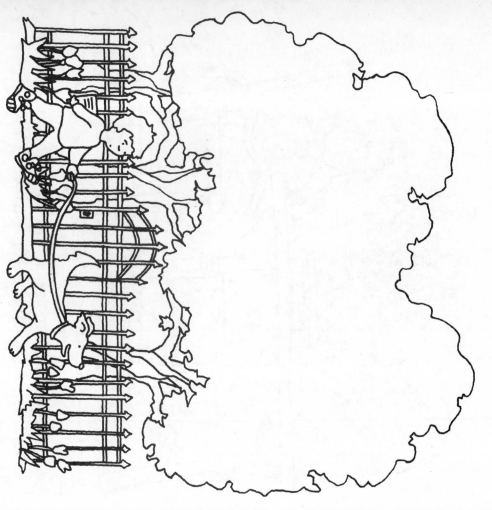

8

Joyce ran back to her house as quick as a mouse. She ran past Howard and Shawn on the lawn. She ran past her father. She ran past her sister and her brother.

"Where's the fire?" asked Mom.

"In my head!" shouted Joyce with joy.

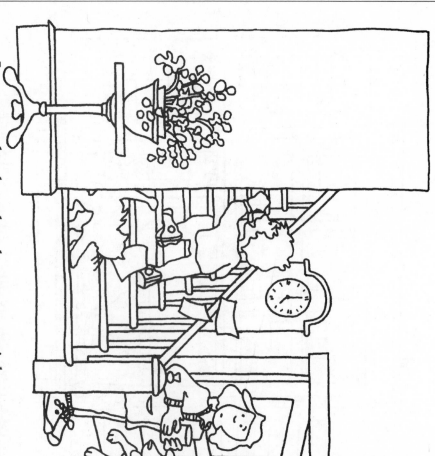

9